THINGS THAT MAKE YOU SAY UHM

(BOOK OF LESSONS, AFFIRMATIONS, QUOTES AND SHORT STORIES)

Genese Darden

Things that make you say Uhm by Genese Darden

Published by Tootsie Collections LLC

https://tootsiecollectionz.myshopify.com/

Copyright © 2022 Genese Darden

All rights reserved. No portion of this book may be reproduced in any form without permission from the publisher, except as permitted by U.S. copyright law. For permissions contact:
tootsiecollectionllc@outlook.com

CONTENT WARNING: this book contains descriptions and vulgar language which may be offensive to some readers and/or inappropriate for children. Reader discretion is advised.

Cover by Jason McFarling
Publishing Mentor: Shuntonese Richardson

Mommy, I promise you they will start saying my name before death.

My dash will count.

Things that make you say, Uhm

A book of lessons, affirmations, quotes, and short stories

Acknowledgements

I dedicate this book to the very ones that put it inside me.

First and foremost all praise and thanks to God, the very reason for my existence and the very one that inspired me, my Pastor, Darius Brooks.

I would like to express my sincere gratitude to my mother, Margo Darden (zanese), and father Charles Marks (Papa Smurf), who always believed in me and pushed me to be great even when I didn't consider myself. Without them I might not be able to complete this masterpiece.

I am extremely grateful to my team that God blessed me with, My children, god-babies and grandchildren; Jemese, Darmese, Zayden, Alaysia, Antwon, Jaden, Amber, Logan, Carisma, Harmony, Tracy, Lil rob, Jermia, James, Anton, Jerry, Wardell, Josiah, Khaleel, Demarco, Treasure, Kemarrion, Tyquan, Shemicka, Amelia, Lexus, Goddess, Dakota, Jordyn and my team of hittas.

My deepest thanks goes to my siblings; Donald, Nirobi, Chanvia, Wayne, Audrey, Iaron, James, Anthony, Darmisha, Genesha, Issiah, Jazz, Sharmeka,Tina, Deontae, Samantha, Laura, Ronnie/pig,Tony,Curtis/pookie, Luke, Latoya,Takeitha, Ieasha, Tommy/wiggy, Jazmon, LilClarence, Anthony/grip, Candyce, Larieda, Frieda and

Kiisha. You all are my source of inspiration. You tell me that I can do anything I put my mind to do.

I also want to appreciate my besties and my cheerleaders; Debra, Danielle, Saquina, Jackie, Kiaishi and to all my family by blood or love rather you a Marks, Jamerson, Darden, Williams, Barrows, Weathers, Lockhart, all luscious ladyz Rip Jaws, Woods, 16th street family, and Lanett families. I also want to acknowledge all my uncles and aunts who were the first to teach me what family was and what it was not, thanks for all your love and support.

I would also like to thank my mentors, Jameela Hooks, Teandra Jackson, Marquita Avery, and Tanzil and to my 2-0 Diane/goddess warrior I look up to you.

My love and appreciation to my hubby Darnell, I love you always and forever.

My gratitude to those who watch over me From heaven; Francess Ann Marks and the three-men that never made me feel nothing far from great, Robert, my uncle/dad, my granddaddy Charles and my uncle Tom. I pray that you will continue to rest in heaven with a smile.

Finally I apologize to all persons who are unnamed and contributed in various ways to bring this work to a success. Thank you all so much.

GENESE DARDEN

Things that make you say uhmmmm....

I could hear my name in my dreams. I at least thought it was one that morning. Beauty, Beauty. The voice remained persistent. Getting up slowly and rubbing what sleep was left in my eyes. I could still hear the persistent name calling. I hurried out of bed and rushed to my window. My sister was outside yelling at me to open the doors to her. I wished she would try to not be so dramatic all the time. This better be good. I swung open the door and asked her to come on in. I turned back and walked towards the kitchen. Do you want some coffee? I would fix you one. I didn't notice that as soon as I opened the door of my house to her, she finally let the tears fall. She seemed reticent. It was not like her to be so quiet when she visits. I finished fixing two cups of coffee and as I looked up to pass her one of it, I saw her face for the first time since I saw her this morning; Tear-stained, bruised and swollen She was pregnant but she had scratches all over her body. 'Baby sister,' I tell her, a vow evident in my tone, 'I am going to kill him. I promise you.' I was filled with rage. 'doesn't care about you or even that we have to see you like this.' 'Calm down, Beautiful.' She said, She never called me by my full name except when she was serious about something. 'I didn't come here to hear you tell me that.' She took a sip of coffee that had been sitting warm in her hand. 'Yes I know you mean well. Beauty, I am done; I am finally tired.' 'Shirley, are you sure you don't want to get yourself some protection?' 'No, I am done, Beauty. I will not stay there again.' She took another sip before continuing. The bruise on her lip caused her to wince. It was quiet but I noticed things like this.

'I think I have been gone mentally for years, but today, I leave physically. The beatings, the women, the children he has outside repeating over and over all these years I am tired, sis.' More tears were flowing at this point. 'My sons are getting bigger—how much longer before they do something about him? I never want to have them to fight my fight.'

'You're right.' I say reaching for her hands. 'Even more because you're pregnant. You have to keep you and your baby safe.' 'Today, it stops for all my loved ones who wanted me out, those that wanted him dead and those that prayed I was not dead. Today I want it for myself. Sis.' 'He came in today smelling of sex and demanded I put my mouth around him. I refused and he saw red. He beat me knowing my kids could hear, knowing they couldn't do anything to save their mother. He beat me because of his insecurities and made-up reasons, but I refuse to suck some other chick off him. My boys cried seeing me that morning, and the girls' eyes were filled with hate for him.

'After dropping the kids off at school he made me ride with him to his mom's house. I felt so bad, and his momma only found reason to justify and begged me to stay with him; she said she loved me, and I know she did, I shared the experience of what his daddy did to her, how could she not love me? I have changed though. She was damaged, and she meant no harm, but I needed air. I was standing on that porch, but I needed air. I needed to go with the wind moving though that porch. So I started to run and run, not knowing where I was headed. I look up, and I am here with you.'

It was quiet in the kitchen where we stood, tears running through her eyes and mine. 'I need you to get the kids from school. I will get our clothes and my car and come here if it is ok, just until I get on my feet.' 'You're welcome here anytime, but come back after getting the clothes. If you are not here when I get back, I will come looking for you.' My sister looked relieved and free of baggage. I have not seen that face in a very long time and it made me ecstatic. When I pulled up to my house with her kids in the backseat, her car was not there, so I headed to her house as I had told her. Throughout the drive there my palms were all sweaty and I couldn't shake the feeling of dread. Pulling to her block, I see so many police cars, an ambulance, and a fire truck. I had hoped that she finally got to his gun and put a whole in him.

Hope was a fickle thing. My Shirley wasn't so lucky. She laid there in the driveway by her trunk. Blood splattered on the clothes she was trying to put in. I could console myself though because I believed she had gone free in a way she hadn't been in years. My little sister will always be a hero and her kids will not lack for a mother. It does just disappoint how sometimes it's too late when you are ready.

Lesson: A lot of Shirleys are out there. They don't all make it when they finally decide to leave. But there's also a lot of Beauties that would very much like to kill the bastard. There's not a lot anyone can do except pray because no one goes until they are truly ready, and when they are, things may not go as well as they planned. There's no big I's, and little U's. Pray for those facing domestic abuse. Most of all, just be there for them and listen; you don't have to say anything at all. Even with every lick I took from my abuser, the lick I took from people hurt harder. They made me feel like my abuser was all I had in the world.

You see, some people are born with strength while others have to build it; never tell them how they should handle it or how you would have handled it, your shoes are different after all. Stop judging and do what you can to help. It doesn't have to be anything more than prayer.

Things that make you say hmmm...

GENESE DARDEN

Value of all ships

Relationships

Friendships

Familyships

Associateships

Situationships

ALL SHIPS

Respect even more

The ships that sails

And the ships that sinks

Some ships are at a standstill

Whatever way your ship

Move to trust it

Embrace it

Learn the lesson

Move in the ship's direction

For your life

Wine for thought

Learn to be passionate about yourself and your dreams

You will win.

To win, make yourself unique to yourself, even if

The world cannot see it

Take on the challenges

And even challenge yourself

Unless you hurting someone to win.

Honesty sets you free

Acceptance allows you to move on.

I know that doing wrong or hurting someone is not always intentional but the thing is that hurting unintentionally or intentionally hurts the same way.

All things require your forgiveness.

Hate stops healing, and in order to receive blessings forgiveness is necessary to prosper, that's why God intervenes because He has forgiven you a million times.

Forgiveness does not mean you have to be friends or allow them back in your circle. Do not get the two mixed up.

What I am about to tell you may turn your stomach or make you not trust me. Maybe even question my loyalty, but if you know me for yourself, you know I am a gentle giant that will never be perfect but worth it. But either way, fuck what you think. I'm human, and I am more significant than the hurt I cause.

This is dedicated to my BFF Kiisha, aka Meme, to those that know the story or think they do, or added fuel to the fire for nothing but the satisfaction of seeing me down. I send my thanks to you.

Here it is from my lips. I slept with my best friend's man, and after this year, unless you read this book, I will never discuss it again. I am done with those hindering me or keeping me down. I am sorry, and whether you believe me or not, I will not repeat it. People always asked me how it started and I never knew why I ever answered them. It was not because they cared but only for the drama. They even wanted to see the number of times and the details.

It should have never happened, and it was wrong on all levels. However, I can't apologize enough, and I have a million times. If no one ever believes you are sorry and God does forgive you that very moment, do not pick it back up after he has forgiven you. It's damaging to your soul. People will never let you live it down or up, for that matter. Accept it and own it. It's only a chapter in your life. Right your wrongs apologize if you hurt someone but move forward and heal. Time waits for no one.

GENESE DARDEN

Even though you are ordinary to people

Be extraordinary to you,

Be a special sauce to yourself.

Keep pushing, God never leaves.

Only you can leave him.

Meditate to feel better

Accept responsibility.

Progress daily through effort.

To become a new you,

You have to become unique and let the old things evaporate.

Winner prescription

To win and become a winner through constant

Learning and growth,

Take a daily dose of winners syrup

Use Medication to think like a winner

#winners' script

#lifetime refills

Value commitment (self-commitment)

Give a 100% daily even when you feel 50%

Do not let fear consume you,

Or let doubts move you.

Teach yourself daily.

I bet you know something about yourself daily.

Give the most significant shot at life every day.

(Effort changes things)

GOD

G = GOD

O = OVER

D = DEMONS

NO MATTER WHAT COMES YOUR WAY

GOOD OR BAD

CRY OUT TO GOD

#PROMISE TO MYSELF

IT TOOK ME DECADES TO BE MYSELF.

I WILL FALL IN LOVE WITH MYSELF DAILY.

I WOULD RATHER DIE THAN LOVE MYSELF LESS.

The Most Dedicated Person to You is Simple

It's you.

Take the loyalty to yourself and smile big.

Be great.

Choose yourself every chance you get.

It will keep you safe and humble.

Damage can be recycled as well as hurt if you allow it to be.

Healing can be recycled as well.

Let's teach healing and confronting those that you need to allow it to happen in your life.

Even though it hurts you to the core, it is only so you can get to the better you.

Whether the person is dead or alive, confronts the hurt or the damage.

Deal with it to overcome the delicate heart.

You have to, and just because they died before you, you have a chance.

To still go to the heavens and confront your monsters.

The weight can still be lifted.

The dead can still be confronted.

I hope this helps someone

And this too;

I love you, yeah you and I believe in you.

GENESE DARDEN

GRANDMA

They say through writing; I could ease the pain of losing you.

I say it does help, but it makes me cry a river.

I never got to tell you I was sorry for leaving you and going to Puerto Rico,

Well, I am truly sorry for leaving you.

Lord knows I saw you lose no fight, so I thought this time was no different.

You were everything I wanted to be.

I never told you I admired the ground you walked on,

And that everything you were, I wanted to be.

I never thanked you for being my grandma and being way more as well; you were my rider, my BFF, my go-to, my shoulder, my mother, aunt, friend, cook, and doctor. You have so many titles, Ms. Lady.

I never told you that after granddaddy, I felt you were all I had left of my dad that could protect me and love me regardless of what the world thought of me.

I never told you that I hold you in the same category as God.

I know no one comes before God, but I didn't know how to separate you two.

THINGS THAT MAKE YOU SAY UHMM

I never admitted I was mad at God for taking you because I knew you wouldn't allow me to think that way.

I still smell you, and it hurts that I could no longer feel you.

I am mad that people moved on. I think they forgot you.

I will never forget you.

I know you love the idea of the family, but it changed, Granny, after you left for home.

I mean, we always talked about a lot of things, and people,

But it is indeed set in stone now.

I wish everybody the best; I have no bad words or things to say.

I hope you are not mad when you die.

I had nothing to prove or hold on to.

I had to stay away from fake love,

You always said keep the family, but granny, I chose me.

I hope you understand that burying you meant I didn't have to accept what I didn't have to.

If God could take you, then it is confirmed that anybody can go.

That never told me nothing that was not good or facts.

GENESE DARDEN

I am going to make you proud even though you are no more.

Guess what, granny I am writing this letter in my book.

I started a tootsie collection in your name.

I am becoming all the great you saw in me even when I have never seen it.

My self-esteem shot up to 100

I'm making big moves that may be small to others.

I feel like I am a big deal.

I'm losing weight, and more than that, I love myself for the first time in years.

Grandma, I hope you are proud of me; I am doing everything I do, for you, granddad and Uncle Dad.

I just want to tell you that I have dug a hole in my heart that can never be filled, and I will never forget you.

I am grateful to have had you in my life, and most of all, I thank you for all you did for us all, even when we did things that hurt you. You never gave up on us, I love you.

No regrets

You served your purpose.

My loves at the time,

You were supposed to do it.

Be blessed, Genese is still here.

Thank God not me.

GENESE DARDEN

Letter to my family

This is a letter to my family,

That became blood relations.

First things first, as I pop the verse

I loved you so bad that it was all bad.

Let me explain, my love for family started at birth

Family meant everything to me

I gave it all I had and it was never enough.

I loved family like a baby I birthed,

Deep.

I go over and beyond to show my gratitude to my family, it killed me to the very core.

As I grew older, I realized it is essential to love the family you make and that blood related doesn't make you family. It has to be said because it's facts.

No one owes me anything but I'm thankful to the people who love me and I am grateful for them.

THINGS THAT MAKE YOU SAY UHMM

I still love my blood relations, and since I know what love is, I'm not mad at those who did not know how.

I am grateful because the bad builds you as much as the good.

I leave you with these; family is everything, but do not be caught up because they share your blood and because you are related they don't owe you love.

Love the family that shows unity by blood or love.

Cherish the family you created and the one you made.

That's the story.

GENESE DARDEN

After I Found Me

I love the way I treat me

I love me

I deserve much more of me

I deserve to fall in love with me

Be bold and beautiful

I see myself as a queen

I am no longer scared to be what I want to be

I am me

Before I Found Me

I am afraid to be what I know I could be

Trapped with pain, even Stevie Wonder could see

Trying to heal with the help of no drugs

When my body urges a pill

Constantly beating me with my failures

When in reality, I am failing me I am afraid to be good to myself.

GENESE DARDEN

If there's a will, there is a way

To press, push, crawl, or walk

Find that thing or person

That gives you a push to keep you

MANIFESTING and growing.

THINGS THAT MAKE YOU SAY UHMM

I never knew how damaged I was until I started

Hurting my kids, the same way

I was damaged

I am sorry.

From a Reconstructing Mom.

Having a conversation with my Rudy, Poop Scoop and Lil G

It makes me go into deep thought,
When you are healing and the person is dead, you still need to confront them.
Especially if the problem or situation stunts your growth
And healing.
I used to think they were dead and there was nothing you could do about it.
I felt if they died and owed you or hurt you,
Then it is over and done with.
You cannot hurt the dead or get anything back from them.
Let them rest in hell.
Nope.
It is never about them. It is about you.
You can still hold them accountable and deal with it.
The pain does not stop because they are dead,
It still has to be dealt with, confronted and forgiven.
Closure is necessary.

THINGS THAT MAKE YOU SAY UHMM

Dead or alive,

It's like you are battling with issues of this person who means everything to you even though he or she raised you.

You have to take away who the person is and what they meant to you.

You have to deal with that person as a woman or man

Person to person

Tell them what broke you or hurt you because the dead can still awaken the hurt buried in you.

Life has no control over your healing, only you do.

GENESE DARDEN

DONEDIDITALL

STILL SAVED

THE ALPHABET GAME DON'T PLAY FAIR

GOD SPARED ME FROM AIDS

THINKING THAT YOU ARE A BOSS OR A BAD BITCH IS NOT ALL IT IS CRANKED UP TO BE.

'Remember every one of your sex partners; you exchange soul ties when having sex with them.'

I hear it all the time, and I thought it was just nuts.

Maybe it was for you, but for the other person, nothing was more important than you (mixed signals, mixed emotions)

All the different partners are draining and draining you on top of adding too much spirits in the soul.

But most of all, life can give you diseases

Some you cannot cure.

Be wise.

I thought I was a beast off four or five pills.

THINGS THAT MAKE YOU SAY UHMM

It gave me a sex drive I was scared of.

I became someone my inner self dreamt of being in the bedroom.

I used to call myself Felicia when I became a different person, when I was not myself.

I could have sex all night and swallow a penis down my throat down to the navel back up and still wanted more.

To God be my witness, I took six niggas of my choice home.

I made them sit and wait in line until I felt it was their turn.

A boss bitch? Please, I was a lost bitch.

I thought I was the doctor or nurse of these niggas

Those were the sex games I played.

I made movies; you had to be there to know.

I was a superhero with sex, or so I thought.

Nearly none of those acts were with condoms

I am being honest to help someone else

A lot of times, I left with nothing but a wet cat

GENESE DARDEN

Even worse, I was given diseases more than once

Thank God they were curable

I had a scare before

Somebody I had sex with told me they had AIDs

Those that slept with him might have contracted AIDs

The whole circle was close to me in multiple ways

I was terrified of going to different places every day taking an AIDs test daily.

Every chance I could

Anxiety should have been my name

My doctors confirmed over and over I was fine

Negative and still is

It could have been me y'all

If only I did life differently

Acting out because the one I loved could not be faithful

I didn't want to be waiting on him and feel stupid

THINGS THAT MAKE YOU SAY UHMM

But what I was feeling now was way worse

I learned my lesson, so no regrets

Pray your guys' body is safe and love yourself beyond measures

Our actions can be death-making decisions

Things that make you say uhm...

Hey young-ins, listen up

When you all say you have one life to live

And you're going to live it,

Be careful.

Because you only have one life is the reason you must be careful living it.

Do not be naive and rebellious,

Or disrespectful,

To your parents or their concerns for your life.

It can have severe consequences if you mishandle them, you will not be blessed accordingly.

Like me, you should be a testimony.

Let's get in tune with treating people accordingly but treat all with respect.

Remember we are survivors not victims.

It could be a lot worse.

THINGS THAT MAKE YOU SAY UHMM

Letters of my heart to two of my heartbeats

Antwon and Jaden,

God already chose you for me to love and raise you.

However, I did not birth you,

But God said you would be mine anyway, I feel as if they came from my womb.

So I thank your birth mom, Jennifer, for being the vessel to deliver my blood sons.

My kings, I love you, and living life without you will be a lousy way to live.

Despite anything you heard of your mom (birth mom), forgive and love her as much as you love me.

You never have to be selfish because nothing in the world will change us

You will always belong to me

I want you to love and forgive her, so you won't become the person

I raised you not to be

GENESE DARDEN

Be responsible

Own the stuff you do wrong

So life won't be hard for you

Antwon, be brave and believe in yourself. Remember, you have a voice

Look people in their eyes when you speak

Mean what you are saying

Stand for what you believe in

Stand up for yourself

Look in the mirror daily

Believe you are handsome and can do anything

Never feel you are not

Get in tune with your emotions

My biggest fear is that you will fear your worth

You will allow others to belittle you

THINGS THAT MAKE YOU SAY UHMM

To take advantage of you

Be strong son and have courage in everything you do

I love you, my second king

Jaden, my 3rd king

My witty, smart, intelligent mouthed baby

You are an amazing king, always

From birth till now, you will be the last one to steal my heart

My soul

You knew what and who you were at 6

I am excited to see what becomes of you in 20 years

If God sees fit for me to see it from the land or the sky

I will be there

I know you will make me proud

You are handsome indeed, a soul snatcher

GENESE DARDEN

Never use your looks to break women down and misuse them

Find that one to love on

Be the man I raised you to be to a woman who is great to you as well

Never treat a woman the way you saw me be mistreated and abused by a man

You didn't like it for me, hate it and even more don't do it to someone else

Be good to people

But be willing to let them go without any revenge

Removing them from your presence will bless your life

If they don't mean you know, then good.

Knock life out, son

I am counting on you to change the world

Love you third king

To all my sons

Zayden, Antwon, Jaden, Tyquan, Darveon, Khaleel, Wardell Lil Jerry, Antwon, Anthony

The love of a son is the greatest gift God could give.

My boys, you are kings

That will rule a nation

You are champions that will conquer all championships moments

That comes your way

I love you all, be more than the streets

Be great leaders

Followers when you have to

Decide when you need to be it

I love you all

GENESE DARDEN

To my first king and only son, I birthed

Remember, mommy loved you from the womb
God chose me to be the special one to carry you
Greatness was growing in my belly
Now 12 years later, you are my everything.
You are so protective of me.
I will appreciate you forever.
You still walk up to me and kiss me.
It makes my soul smile.
Throughout life, and I do hope God blesses me to see it
Be you
It is alright to be different and to like other things
People may not understand
You are unique and different
I knew that from the womb
You embraced into this world early but so strong
The year you were born was challenging for me
I endured and lost so much that year you were born
You were the only good thing that came that year and you were all I needed

THINGS THAT MAKE YOU SAY UHMM

Be your brother's keeper. They look up to you

But most of all, cry when you want

Never let anybody tell you it is not manly

It is the best thing about becoming a man

Having emotions means you are human

Be brave and strong

Keep being one of the best chapters of my life

Bud, as I call you

You are part of the puzzle that fits imperfectly perfectly in my life.

I Love my first king

GENESE DARDEN

Laysia the 3rd princess of the bunch

You have so much in you that you don't even know

You are unique and smart

Life has not dealt you the greatest storms

But you were blessed to be part of a great family

I thank God for you daily

I want you to see life as good and you can be anything you want to be

Take your pain and put power in it, to be the greatest story ever to grace the world

You are complicated and hard-headed at times; you rock and abuse every nerve I have

I wouldn't have it any other way

I will always be here for you; even after I die I will become your angel.

I want you to be great at whatever the future holds

Be the best you can be

THINGS THAT MAKE YOU SAY UHMM

Remember everything I ever did to you, good or bad, was because I loved you.

And I thought those decisions were the greatest to do

Be great, my princess

GENESE DARDEN

The story of incest, drugs, confusion, death and still no regrets

The things that happen at 6134 s Whipple will definitely make you say, Uhm.

But it built me into who I am today.

Testimony time,

Get the wine.

Well, at that address, I learned that I could be somebody else.

I thought I had morals until they were tested.

Well, living the fast life will always make you go against things you believe in strongly.

Facts it was so much fucking and orgasms at that address;

Drugs, parties, and plenty of grief.

We lost badly those years.

I lost homies back to back,

Major street wars that changed us all,

THINGS THAT MAKE YOU SAY UHMM

I was a true drinker and pill poppin animal.

That was the new me,

I turned out to be the life of the party trying to be the life of the party,

I would later wish I never went to, well not ever went to but made better decisions

Amongst it all, God still covered me.

It was a good thing

Man I gained a brother for life

My "Dundee" as I call him

That was God's way of saying I will still send you an angel

Even when I was disappointing him

Like I said previously, it was a lot of drugs.

These drugs took men in and out of beds.

Which led me to damage relationships and later led to a lot of souls searching and

And boy did it test who I was.

GENESE DARDEN

In one of my many party nights, I, yes me ate my sister /1st cousin pussy

With her then man

She says she was asleep when we were doing it, I recall different

But whether it's her truth you believe or mine it happened.

I was off drugs and pills and a nut is what I needed

How I got it never mattered and I was not in that room which was mine on no bully shit

I was invited

I do recall all us in that room with another cousin by love not blood but family all the same

We were doing things as usual, not the first time I had been nowhere.

With her naked and fucking

She always wanted to quit or say yuck after the first but was down from the start

Unless she felt he was fucking someone better than her

Not because I was fat and ugly or ugly shaped, so she say

THINGS THAT MAKE YOU SAY UHMM

Because if that was so, how the fuck did we all did it before with another one of my cousins and we all were burning

That's another story though

She always got something bad to say about me, for that matter

ANYBODY BUT HER WORD ALWAYS RAN MY FAMILY SO I NEVER RUSHED TO TELL MY SIDE

If it was snowing and she said it was raining, they believed it till this day

That's why I move different now

But I own what I did

I am grown, I ate my sister cousin pussy

She will never let me forget that

Matter of fact she has so many demons and fucked up ways she never let me

Forget the bad in this life

She holds it to hurt people

GENESE DARDEN

She was the issue

Always justified her stupidity and everybody went with it, cool

I decided she will not keep doing it to me

So yes I did it

Even when the argument is something else she brings it up cool

I was a monster then. I did a lot of shit. I had no business or was nasty as fuck.

I apologize if I hurt someone but I hurt me the most

Today that shit want hurt me anymore

Because I am moving forward

But at that same address and room, she fucked one of my favorite big cousins that is blood as well.

But destroying me for the same mistake she made. The kettle calling the pot black

Things that make you say uhm, right

Get the fuck out of here

THINGS THAT MAKE YOU SAY UHMM

It stops here

The moral of this is cleansing for me, and you can never hurt me again, the world knows.

You have to admit your wrongs and grow from it

Never forget it is a double edge sword

The act was gross,

Incest nasty,

I learned my lesson.

You still cannot allow a person to continue to hold something over you

God forgave you already

Especially when they know what you did.

Another lesson;

Never be ashamed of what you did, good or bad when it changed you to be better.

Even if it destroyed you, it was a chapter in your life and you got back up.

Make another chapter a better one

GENESE DARDEN

See, Nesa cannot run from Nesa

And I sure won't let a human being keep humiliating me for something that I did

I apologized, and God forgave me.

I heard it all

Fat, plus-sized, big momma, obese, extra-wide, bigger than me

I heard it all

The people I heard it from the most were blood majority of the time

Funny, I've always been a plus-sized woman

God chose me to be this

Who could possibly be this big and great as me, this fantastic big girl

What people miss is that I was plus-sized in my goals as well

My dreams, I had fat plans great big, mother

With a great big heart

A significant amount of love to give

Chasing fat bags

A skinny girl could never live this life meant for B.I.G NESA.

GENESE DARDEN

Nobody knows a man better than the woman living with him

And I do mean nobody, not his momma, daddy, best friend, brother ,sister

Nobody

That nigga gives a front or one side of the story

But the woman

His woman

She sees it and get the real him

The raw and unfiltered ,broken but healing, loving but hateful at times, crazy but caring, unstable but functioning, controlling but yet protective psychopath

So do not tell her he does not like that. I don't believe it.

My moral of it all

Stay out of relationship business because it damages good relations with good people because you believe something and you are not there.

And most of the time, they will be back together. Your messiness had nothing at all to do with your point.

GENESE DARDEN

You are allowed to be both a masterpiece and a work in progress

Do not be afraid to do so

Be everything you learn along the way.

THINGS THAT MAKE YOU SAY UHMM

I gave them wings and they taught me to fly.

Letter to my daughters; Tracy, Amber, Carisma, Jemese ,Alaysia, Amora, Shemicka

I want you all to know mommy, god-mama loves you all dearly. Every lesson I learned is to teach it to you all. All lessons I learned were not always wise and were always not intended to be learnt that way, but I learned anyway. You should know I have made my fair share of mistakes and I have also learned from them. I know there are some lessons you will also learn on your own as well and I ask God to protect you, during those times.

Promise to listen when others try to help you or give you advice. If it's genuine and they are concerned about you and your wellbeing, listen. Watch people's life lessons. Do not judge but learn from them or grow from them. Be whatever you want to be, whoever you need to be as long as you have no regrets and can live with them. If there are doubts or regrets, you should avoid doing it. Follow your heart and mind the first time it registers to your initial moment.

Be a voice; just don't listen to the voice inside of you.

Whenever you fail, be grateful and grow because whatever happened was meant to happen in your life. God chooses you for the battle, just embrace the lesson. I know as your parent, I have failed y'all and I have been wrong in a million ways even when I thought I was right. I apologize because it was a traditional way I was taught by the parents who raised the parents and me before them. Of course, I thought it was also right. I only tried to be the best mom you guys had, but I was also human. I like to think we grew together as I helped you grow and mature as children.

As I was getting older, I just knew you. I loved you guys more than anything I ever could love. I can be a jerk or even a bully at times. I can work your nerves as well as you do mine.

But always remember, nothing will stop me from loving you guys

THINGS THAT MAKE YOU SAY UHMM

Jemese,

I want you to know you were my first everything. From the moment you were growing in my womb, I knew you were great. I have high expectations for you. I know you were going to be great from the beginning. I never knew love like this as I looked into your dreamy eyes. The first time I carried you, you were perfect and unique. I thank God for you daily. I see so much of you in me, even the hidden parts of me. I never allowed anyone to see. I love your courage to stand your ground and what you believe in. I love your dedication and loyalty to those you love and how you will go over and beyond to show you give them support. You are feisty but a protector at the same time. You are always mama's ride or die chick.

I want you to know you're my hero. You saved me from myself. I did not wish to see you in this world without me, and I am the cause because I ended my life. Thank you for allowing me to be your mommy through the good and bad. Thank you for being the best daughter and sister and standing in place as their second mom sometimes when I am working to provide or when the world seems overwhelming at times. You have been more to me than you had to be and I appreciate you. I pray for you daily throughout the day. I pray for those places you hurt that I do not know about. Let the hurt build you. Promise never to

GENESE DARDEN

forget me in this world as kids do when they get older. Give me flowers while I am here. When you go into the world as a young adult, always make time to check on me. Rudy I am very proud of you, even if I do not tell you enough. You are a diamond, and I am blessed to have you, Rudy. Your ambition is over the top. I have no doubt how great your future will be and what great things will happen in your life.

Mommy will always be your cheerleader and greatest support. Take everything they say you couldn't have and get everything you want in this world. Again I love you, Rudy.

Darmese.

The second storm to come out of my womb. I thank God for you as you turn 17 this year 2021. I cried all day because my baby was growing up, gracing the world so perfectly. I knew the time was coming which caused so much fear. I want to protect you forever. The world is so different and scary now. I want you to be alert and wise in everything you do or say. Be watchful and pray wherever you go. Love and be kind. There are still good people in the world. You make sure you stay one of those people. I love your ambition and stubbornness. I love you for always being a leader. I love how you don't follow the wrong things others do. Never be scared to be a follower baby just recognize when you have to be one. My concern for you is to stop holding in your pain and hurt and emotions and practice healing. I don't want you to be 41 like me and just begin to heal and face your problems. I apologize to you and the other siblings if I ever hurt you deeply but I can assure you it wasn't my intention.

You should know, I am working to be the best version of myself. I never want to be the cause of your pain but every bit of the reason for your healing.

Stand your ground and never let people push you over. I will always be your biggest fan. I can see you being the prettiest traveling nurse you can be and being great at whatever you do. You've got the Midas touch. Livy I am proud of you and so ready to see you grace that stage in June. Remember I am always here even when God calls me home.

I will be the wind beneath your feet.

THINGS THAT MAKE YOU SAY UHMM

I realize people would rather die before they do these 7 things:

1. Make a mistake and apologize
2. Say thank you
3. Ask questions when they are confused
4. Ask for help when they are stuck
5. Admit when they wrong
6. Give without reservations
7. Tell someone you love; 'I love you'. Tell them now while they are in the world. It doesn't mean much when they are gone.

Let change begin with you. You are accountable for how you react or respond to things. All things do not deserve a response or reaction.

GENESE DARDEN

Rubbing my head always sends me into the past

As I feel the gash in my head with a touch, I am reminded of the lessons life has taught me.

It is important to note, everybody in this life would not be treated equally. You can give your kid the name of a person you hold to high standards and they will be the very one to hurt you. It taught me to not get into kids' mess so fast.

Most adults can be wrong as hell. My cousin and I had a conflict and my aunt jumped in to fight me. She busted my head in the process. This gave me funny feelings for so long. That was the very first day I felt like I did not belong in the family. It was a long traumatic experience that I carried for a long time. I never knew why this happened; they never apologized and life went on.

I remembered being scared to be with them when my grandma was not there. They would jump on me, it was lonely. My mom was not there to defend me and my dad was incarcerated. I wanted her to love me so bad that I made a fool of myself. I remembered her calling me medusa and they would all laugh. I wanted to pretend that it didn't hurt. I would mask my pain by telling jokes; it was my way of coping with the hurt. Whenever It was snowing outside; my aunt would make me go to the store while her kids were sitting in the warmth. I would cry on the way to the store and hurry up and when I get back home I would pretend as if nothing happened.

They would always hit me with "you the oldest," and God, I hated it.

I would hurt and being the oldest I had to swallow up the shit they threw at me. I took the punk way out all the time, because I was told the biggest lie, that family is all you need when in life. Now I know family is not always the one you need. Blood makes you related but family is who you make it. Many times I took licks from family verbally and physically and sucked it up when I rather smacked them to the floor. You must stand up for yourself. Well, I am healed now, and she was not all bad all the time. It was just the times she did hurt me I was damaged.

She taught me a lot, even about these streets, but even to this day I knew I wasn't her favorite.

As an adult now, I have come to realize It is what it is. All is well with us now. I have forgiven and healed. I am still thankful she played a part in my life, good or bad. As I got older, I became close to her daughter. One thing I know is that when you cannot forgive wholeheartedly, it will be

GENESE DARDEN

hard to have a relationship with that person. Things are crazy as hell, but hey, those are the things that make you say, "Hmmm

Do not lose focus

Today I heard from a man as I was scrolling through my Facebook timeline.

"Protect your focus like you will your home, car, kids or anything important."

If you are around people that are distracted, you will be distracted. When you focus, protect it. You will be able to protect yourself from people who you wouldn't talk to when you are focused. You wouldn't be found in a mess when you are focused.

Stay focused y'all, and protect it. Anything that tries to steal or distract you has got to move out of your way.
#clear and focus

GENESE DARDEN

Daddy's broken princess

7/14/80 was the day I was born, and the day the first man I saw called me his princess. His firstborn is really his third child. I lost one of my brothers, who died before I was born. I also had another brother whose name is Wayne but he was not allowed in our life. I always knew of him, but his mother wanted something different for him, she wanted him to be raised by another man and denied my father in his life.

So here I was, or so I thought. Only a few people can recall their childhood memories and I was one of the few. I could remember his love and how it felt and when he was jailed, I was told his love. I could recall when I was taken to visit him in jail and he would hold me in his arms, my King, my happy place.

My Daddy's parents made sure to always be in my life. They assisted my mother in raising me. I was happy knowing I was his princess. His incarceration damaged me. I longed for him to be home because my cousins used to tease me about him. Kids can be cruel, especially the ones who had a dad that was physically able to do things for them or be at events with them. I remember my cousin used to say my daddy was in jail for stealing a sucker out of a baby mouth. I was really naive as a child, and I cried so hard.

The only exception was for my uncle Robert and his kids; he always made me feel I had him. He used to say, "I am to you what my brother cannot be in the physical sense." He lived that down till his death. His death still hurts. He was my uncle and father in many ways that my own daddy wasn't. After about 12 years, I might have been 12 or 13 years old, my dad was released from jail. It felt like Christmas to me. I was so happy because all the things I dreamt about doing with my pops would now become a reality. At least that was what I thought; until I went from a princess who thought things were finally changing to a broken princess facing a new reality.

My granddaddy retired. His first son came home and he handed over all his business to him, and in no time, the business failed. All my granddaddy had worked for, was lost. I resented them, but I was just a kid, so there was nothing I could do.

We lost everything they worked hard for, but most of all, I lost my dad to the streets and drugs. I became burdened with his hardships. I never felt close to him when he came home. And even when I tried, I always felt like I was never enough.

I became the parent and I had to save him especially when others wanted to hurt him because of the drugs. I was just daddy's little princess so I even fed the monster of addiction that was causing him to fade. Till this day, he has never told me he loved me, until I said it first.

My dad's actions were not healthy and maybe he felt I was not the best daughter but our bond was never there no matter how much I tried. He showed his kindness to others but I never got to experience it. Maybe he just didn't know how to be.

I gradually became immune. His incarceration left him clueless and he knew nothing about fatherhood and what it entails. I always made excuses for why he was this way but it never healed my pain. I was my daddy's broken princess at the end of the day. I had to become responsible for myself and let him be responsible for himself.

He did not want me to ever accept things from a man and tell me how they should be treated but he never taught me what one is. Being manipulated and played on was first initiated by my dad.

Fathers, show your daughters their worth and how she is supposed to be treated. Majority of the time, she finds you in the man she picks. I saw my father mistreat good women and say cruel things to women. He made me a subject for low self esteem by his constant reference to my weight. He reminded me in ways that he thought it did not hurt.

Papa Smurf always said, "I do not like big women, but for some money or something. They may even have good pussy but none will be caught with me. I just do not like big women. That is why God blessed me with a big daughter."

People, fathers, Uncles, men, women, mothers, and aunts, watch what you say to your children, nieces or nephews. It could kill their souls and break their heart and you would never know it.

I saw how he let a good woman go, and I backed away from my relationship with her because I felt terrible about the way handled it. He focused on her weight not her heart and everything she helped him with as a man. She was beautiful, but he said he just couldn't date big women. Think how that made me feel. I watched him treat his nieces better than me, not equal better. They could be playing; you know horsing around with him. I would do the same thing and he went crazy on me. He would Say;

"Do not play with me."

And I would say, "They were just playing with you."

"They are not my daughter, stop playing with me."

He would be so mad at me for waking him up early to help around the house but he would cook for one of his nieces because she was sick. Things that made me say hmmm.

My other siblings felt like I had my dad more than them. They didn't know the half. I had just as much of him as they did, if not less. Regardless of what he did or didn't do he was still my Papa Smurf and my world. I forgive him for everything as God forgave me for a million things, despite what he was to me he was a great granddad he didn't miss a beat. Maybe that was his way of saying I am sorry, I am better and I am fixing me. He is doing great now and he is human, he is not perfect, he is still here. I forgive him a hundred percent, so I can move on. I am and will always be his princess and I let the broken pieces fall off because I am fixed by God's stripes.

I pray for healing and all the places I do not know about or I cannot fix.

I love my papa Smurf and most importantly I love me enough because I am enough.

Give it your all every day

You will get enough sleep when you die.

Remember giving 99% is the same as 0%

GENESE DARDEN

Do not regret anything you did for people

You gave them the best you had to give them

They didn't appreciate it.

That's on them, not you.

You owe it to yourself to put you and your life first.

Block negativity and fake people and love and Cherish the real ones

Do not let go of you.

GENESE DARDEN

When this question comes up; am I even enough or am I worthy?

SAY HELL YES, IF YOU BELIEVE YOU COULD, YOU CAN.

THINGS THAT MAKE YOU SAY UHMM

When you see their spirit wrong,

Run

And treat people accordingly

Whoever they are.

GENESE DARDEN

When you break family generational curses,

They will cast you out

And make you feel like the black sheep

When really, you are actually the damn GOAT!

If I ever sit down and confide in you,

It's so you can understand why I am who I am now

And who I was before.

GENESE DARDEN

If my circle isn't trying to better themselves,

In any way,

I have to find a new circle.

I learned that people hate to see you reach the top

I learned that when someone says something good about you, people bring up all the bad that were in the past. They give the worst version of you to people. They give them more to be mad at. You must keep moving forward because when they knock on that old door, you will no longer be inclined to answer it. You will tell them to fuck off and shut the fuck up, never give them the fucks they need.

GENESE DARDEN

Judge me when you become perfect and that will never be.

Healing does not mean the mess did not happen,

But it means that it no longer consumes you.

GENESE DARDEN

Remember

Give it your best shot

99% percent is the same as 0%

MY TALK WITH MY OLD MAN.

Me: I want more pops, why can't I have it?

God: Wanting is a plan without action. If you want more, you have to take action to get it.

Me: God, I am so hurt. I am angry all the time because of the things I've been through, the hand that life has dealt me, the experience that I felt I didn't deserve to go through and the ones who hurt me.

God: Trust me and only me, first and foremost. Heal the heart from the hurt as well as the ones who caused you to hurt. You forgive for yourself, not for them. Be grateful for my lessons.

Me: I am not worthy of anything, it feels like I was born a tragedy

God: Everything I created is by far a tragedy that is meant to be great. You are more than you think of yourself, say it and believe the power is in the tongue and manifest. Be careful with your words, I build you for excellence.

GENESE DARDEN

EVERYTHING

Me: I failed me, (tears falling)

God: let your tears drop no more, my child. It is alright. Your father is here with his shoulders to lean on. You failed at nothing. Your time is not my time. That is, it. You can plan great things, but you have to plan with me, not without me.

MORAL: Never think you failed because you were not aligned with God. When you plan, ask God to go ahead of you and prepare. He is always with you every step of the way.

Things that make you say, Uhm

A book of lessons, affirmations, quotes, and short stories

About the Author

Genese Darden is a 41 year old mom, friend, sister, aunt, associate, wife and more. She is an Author, Tax Preparer, and Insurance agent with both her Associate and Bachelors Degree in Criminal Justice. She is a God-fearing woman who truly believes that no weapon formed against her will prosper.

Follow the Author and stay tuned for Part 2

Facebook: @Ceogenese Darden

Instagram: @Ceogenesedarden

Website: www.tootsiecollectionz.myshopify.com

www.ingramcontent.com/pod-product-compliance
Lightning Source LLC
Chambersburg PA
CBHW031637160426
43196CB00006B/460